WAY TO PLAY

MW00581716

FREE Downloadable Recordings!

Intermediate

Mark Tonelli
Philip Groeber

The perfect supplemental book for students using
Everybody's Jazz Guitar Method 1 or any other Jazz Guitar Method
AND for the jazz guitarist who desires to learn the beauty
of playing chord melody!

Contents

Production: Frank Hackinson
Production Coordinator: Philip Groeber
Editor: Philip Groeber
Cover Design: Andi Whitmer

Engraving: Tempo Music Press, Inc.
Printer: Tempo Music Press, Inc.
Recording Credits: Mark Tonelli (guitar)
Photo Credit: Eastman Guitar (page 18)

THE F·J·H MUSIC COMPANY INC.

Frank J. Hackinson

ISBN-13: 978-1-61928-256-8

About this Book

The ability to play the chords and the melody of a song at the same time is one of the unique features of the guitar. In jazz guitar, it's known as "chord melody." Chord melody transforms the guitar into a one-man band: you play the melody, accompany, provide the bass line, and define the time.

The purpose of this book is twofold:

1. provide specific instruction on how to create your own chord melodies (pages 3-7)
2. show you the inner workings of chord melody through 13 jazz guitar songs in a variety of styles. (pages 8-29)

Each song has been carefully arranged to help you understand and learn about the basic parts of a chord melody. Right-hand technique requires hybrid picking or fingerpicking (classical style).

Melody

The melody is the main tune of a song, the singable part. Without the melody, there is no "melody" in chord melody. Typically, the melody is played "on top," that is, as the highest note in a chord, usually on the highest two strings, E or B. It's important to bring out the melody and not let it get lost in the chord.

Inner Voices

The inner voices form the middle part of the chord. They usually fall on the 2nd-5th strings. They often include the critical 3rds and 7ths, which define chord quality (major, minor, dominant, diminished, and half diminished). The inner voices can also include 5ths or 6ths as well as color tones, 9ths, 11ths, and 13ths. Without the inner voices, there is no "chord" in chord melody.

Bass

The bass forms the foundation of a chord. Without the bass, the inner voices or even the melody may not make sense. In particular, when the bass note is the root of the chord, as is often the case, it places the chord tones in context. Because, when we refer to a 3rd or 6th or 11th, what we are really saying is that chord tone is a 3rd or 6th or 11th above the root. Thus, it's the relationship between the bass note as root and other chord tones that defines them. The bass note is usually played on the 5th or 6th and occasionally on the 4th string.

Interpretation

There are other elements that contribute to the making of a great chord melody: rhythm, articulation, dynamics, and tempo.

Harmony

Here are three ways in which jazz harmony is created in this book.

Extensions and Altered Notes Extensions (9's, 11's, and 13's) and altered notes ($\flat$9, $\sharp$9, $\flat$11, $\sharp$11, and $\flat$13) are the basic ways to add color to triads and seventh chords. They give jazz its characteristic lush harmonic quality.

Substitution A common chord substitution is the "tritone sub." The basic premise is to substitute a chord— generally a dominant 7th— one tritone away. For example, if G7 is the original chord, resolving to C, then the tritone sub would be D$\flat$7($\flat$5), as D$\flat$ is a tritone away from G.

Reharmonization Occurs when the original chord has been replaced or reharmonized with a completely new, sometimes unrelated chord that may fall outside the home key.

Learn even more about chord melody using *Way To Play Jazz Guitar: Riffs and Chord*s (G1052).

G1056

How to Build a Chord Melody

Before you begin playing a full chord melody, we are going to show you how to build one from the ground up, one step at a time. To do this, we will use the first four bars of the simple and universally familiar nursery rhyme, *Twinkle, Twinkle, Little Star*. Jazz musicians refer to this song as *Twinkle*. You can use this method of building a chord melody or a variation of it for any future chord melody you might create.

TWINKLE

Step 1 - Melody in concert pitch

Find a reliable source. As the title of this step suggests, the melody is written in concert pitch. The harmony is indicated above the staff using "chord symbols." Use the original harmony on your source.

Step 2 - Melody up an octave.

The guitar, however, is a "transposing" instrument. That means when you play the written note on the music, that note "sounds" one octave lower. To illustrate, think of the note Middle C on the piano. On the treble clef staff, Middle C is written just under the staff, with one ledger line. But when a guitarist plays this note, the note that sounds is actually one octave lower. So for a guitarist to play a note that sounds like a concert pitch Middle C, the guitarist must play that note one octave higher, third space on the treble clef staff. In turn, for all notes played on the guitar to sound in concert pitch, the guitarist must transpose every note up one octave. That's what we've done in Step 2.

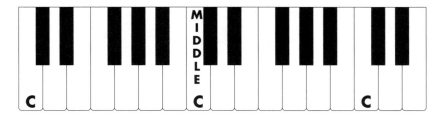

Another reason to transpose the melody up an octave before creating a chord melody is that a melody in concert pitch tends to be played on the lower strings. This does not leave you enough strings to build a full chord below the melody, which we'll begin doing in the following steps. As you progress, the location of these notes on the fingerboard may change.

Step 3 - Add the root to each chord.

With the melody in the proper octave, we slowly begin to add the harmony. A simple and effective way to start this process is to play the melody and the root of each chord. The "harmonic rhythm" (the rate at which chords change)— is typically on beats 1 and/or 3 in traditional jazz.
By playing the melody with the root, you will get a sense of the harmonic rhythm and begin to hear a shell of the harmony. In addition, this will enable you to begin the process of playing multiple notes at once and help you build up to larger chords.

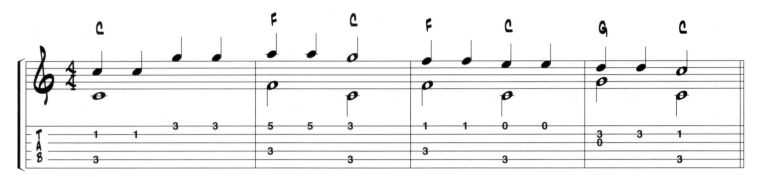

As your progress through the following steps you may find the root note you chose might work better in a different octave. Make any adjustments you feel are necessary.

Step 4 - Fill in the chords.

In this step, we keep the bass note and melody and begin to fill in the inner voices to create full chords. Notice that the melody from Steps 2-3 has been perfectly preserved as the highest pitch, "on top," an important step. You will also see that we moved the root up an octave in the C chord in bar 2, to make the chord a little easier to play. We also changed the location of the F root to make the F chord easier to play. You will continue to see the locations of some chords shift to accommodate changes we will make.

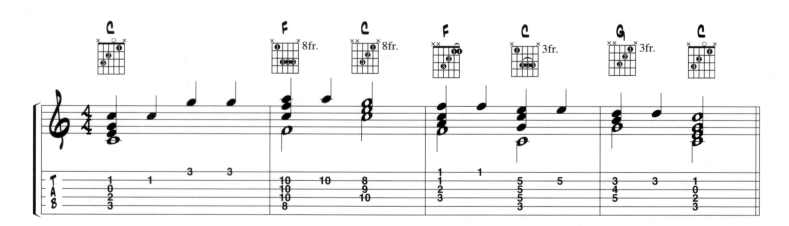

4

Step 5 - Add sevenths.

The triads (three-note chords) in Step 4 gave us the basic harmony. Now we flesh them out a little with 7ths, giving us four notes per chord in some cases and adding a hint of color. You will see that the Fmaj7 chord no longer has the root as the lowest note of the chord (the bass note.) The 7th, E, is now the bass note. This is fine, because the root is still present in the melody, so we get a full seventh chord. The E bass provides a pleasing dissonance which is resolved on beat 2.

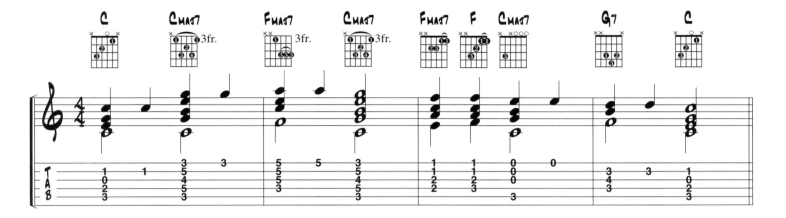

Step 6 - Add color tones.

Even with seventh chords in place, we still lack the vibrant color of jazz. So in this step, we add more color by including notes above the basic seventh chords— 9s, 11s, and 13's. These notes are called extensions, because they "extend" the basic harmony. Specifically, we removed the 7th and added a 6 and a 9 to the Cmaj7 chord in bar 2, making it a C 6/9. We also added a 9th, an A, to the G7 chord in bar 4, making it a G9.

In this step, we do have a chord that is actually missing the root, the C6/9. It's "rootless." This is common in jazz, particularly when performing with a bassist, who will often play the root. Even without a bassist playing the root, however, enough of the chord tones are often present that the ear "fills in" the root or other missing chord tones that can be omitted in certain cases.

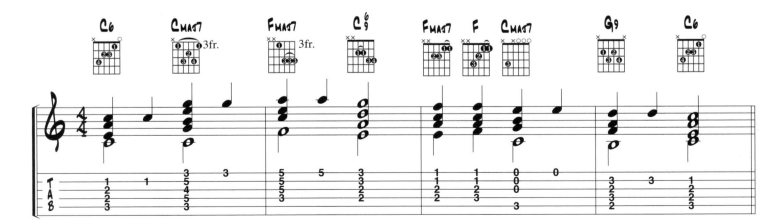

Step 7 - Reharmonize and alter extensions.

This last step completes the chord melody and gives us the final version. We didn't really change much from Step 4, but what we did requires a little explanation.

In bar 2, we "reharmonized" the chords, meaning that we changed the original chord of Cmaj7 to an A7($\flat$9) (rootless). In addition, we changed the chord on the downbeat of bar 3 from Fmaj7 to Dm7. We did this because A7 is a dominant chord (V7), and in traditional jazz harmony, dominant chords like to "resolve" to the I chord, the home chord: A7 (V7) to D (I). Reharmonization is also a common jazz practice and is another way of adding color to a piece and giving it a more authentic jazz sound.

Also, in bar 4 we "altered" the 9th of G7, an A, and made it an A$\flat$. Extensions, particularly on a dominant chord, like the G7, can usually be raised or lowered, providing an additional avenue of color.

When you compare the final version with where we started, you can hear a real evolution!

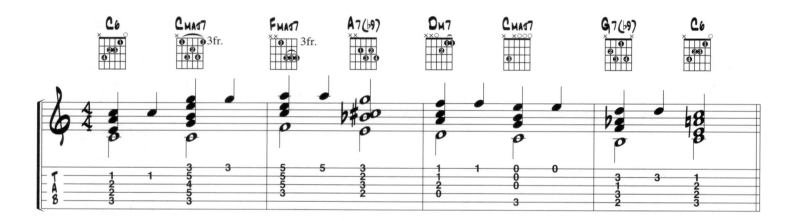

Now look on page 7 for the complete *Twinkle* chord melody arrangement.

When working on your own composition/arrangement, play it many, many times. If you are not quite pleased with the harmonies you created, review your choices and make changes. Creating a chord melody is a long and detailed process.

We hope you have enjoyed learning the many techniques necessary for creating a chord-melody for the long-time favorite *Twinkle*. In the following pages you will be playing many more beautiful melodies. Be sure to analyze the arrangements for the techniques you have learned while studying *Twinkle*.

Let's go!

TWINKLE

TRADITIONAL

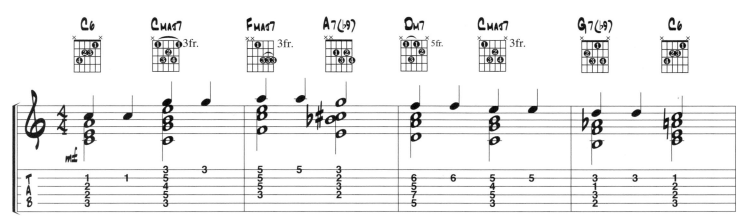

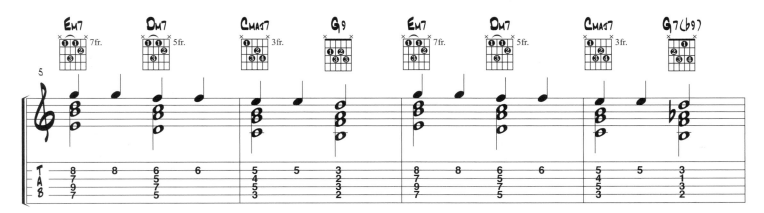

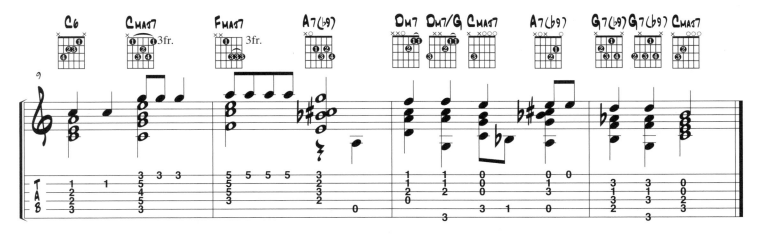

G1056

TIME TO GET BUSY!

Here are two more examples to help illustrate how this musical transformation works. Analyze these tunes using the *Seven Steps of How to Build a Chord Melody* you learned in the previous pages.

You will find that there is much more to this process than the Seven Steps; there is a lot creativity going on. You will see additional chord changes being added, chords with bass notes other than the root, bass lines moving in step-wise motion, chord changes anticipating the beat, using pitches that are outside of the scale, the addition of counter melodies, etc.

At this point we encourage you to begin creating your own chord melodies from music that you like to play and listen to. Don't choose difficult tunes to start with. With a little research you can find many songs that will be good for you to begin your journey, especially in the *Americana* genre. Start your arrangements by grabbing your manuscript book and get going! If you can, input your manuscript into your favorite music notation program. Record your completed arrangement when it is the way you like it.

Here is a quote from Joe Pass, a famous jazz guitarist known for his chord melody skills, "Guitarists should be able to pick up the guitar and play music on it for an hour, without a rhythm section or anything!"

Time to get busy!

AURA LEE
(LAST FOUR MEASURES)

TRADITIONAL

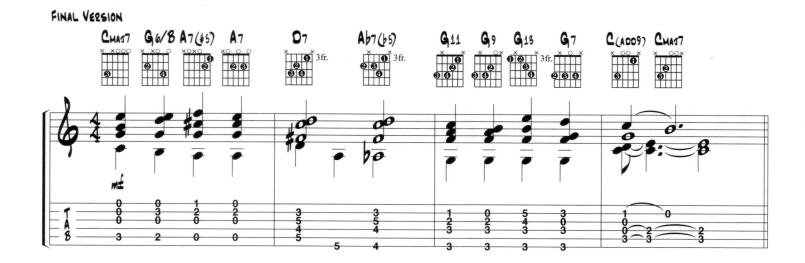

G1056

JAZZ MOOD

PHILIP GROEBER

Jazz Mood uses the *Seven Steps* outlined in this book to create a chord melody.

The arrangements in the rest of the book are in approximate level in order of difficulty.

Greensleeves

Traditional

G1056

Shenandoah

Traditional

G1056

Silent Night

Lyrics by Joseph Mohr
Music by Franz Gruber

Relaxed ♩=100

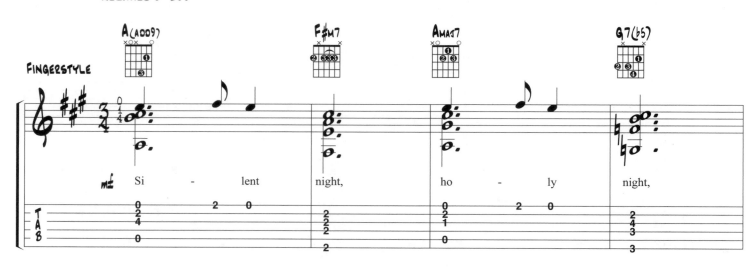

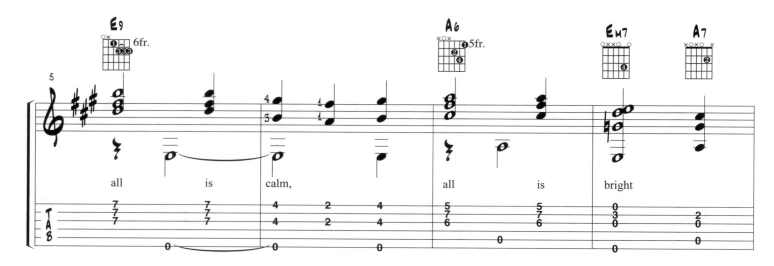

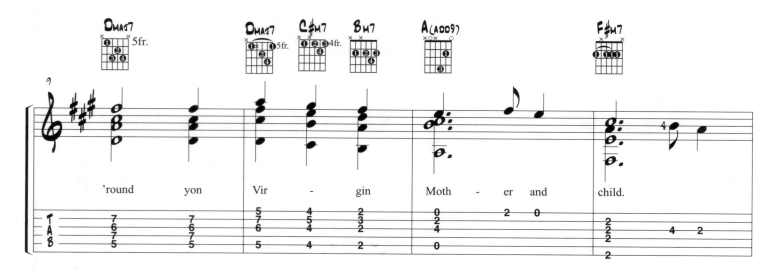

G1056

Swanee River

Stephen Foster

G1056

Selected list of chord melody classics

It's so important to hear what this music sounds like! So we've included a list of classic recordings that feature great chord melody work by master jazz guitarists. Some of the recordings are under the guitarist's own name, while other recordings include the guitar as an accompanist to the bandleader (the leader is indicated in parentheses). Most of the recordings feature the guitarists in the context of a band, but some are solo guitar recordings. As well, many of these recordings showcase the guitarist's ability to improvise and comp for other soloists, so listen for that, too.

Peter Bernstein - Solo Guitar: Live At Smalls

Ed Bickert - *Like Someone in Love* (with Paul Desmond)

Kenny Burrell - *A Night at the Vanguard*

Ted Greene - *Solo Guitar*

Jim Hall - *Jazz Guitar; Alone Together* (a duo with bassist Ron Carter); *The Bridge* (with Sonny Rollins)

Gilad Hekselman - This Just In

Barney Kessel - *The Poll Winners*

Lage Lund - Idlewild

Wes Montgomery - *The Incredible Jazz Guitar; A Dynamic New Sound: Guitar Organ Drums*

Joe Pass - Misty

Joe Pass - *Virtuoso; Finally* (a duo with bassist Red Mitchell)

Adam Rogers - Sight

Kurt Rosenwinkel - Deep Song

Johnny Smith - *Moonlight In Vermont*

Mike Stern - *Standards and Other Songs*

Eastman Guitar Model ER4
Mark Tonelli plays a ER4 and is an Eastman Guitar Artist.

G1056

TO A WILD ROSE

Edward MacDowell

Slowly with expression ♩=72

G1056

19

Amazing Grace

John Newton

G1056

As Summer Leaves

Philip Groeber

G1056

C&R Blues

Mark Tonelli

G1056

NINE MILES FROM HOME

Mark Tonelli

G1056

Performance Notes

Amazing Grace

Amazing Grace comes from the American gospel tradition. This arrangement fleshes out the original harmony, which is mostly in triads, and adds extensions and altered notes above the basic chord tones. In essence, anytime there's a 7, 9, 11, or 13 in a chord symbol, the harmony has been expanded. The first half of the melody, bars 1-16, has the melody in a lower octave, and the second half of the melody (bars 16-30) transposes it up one octave.

The final three bars feature a standard of gospel literature— the "plagal" cadence, that is the IV chord resolving to the I chord, in this case fleshed out with 7ths. Here the IV chord is Fmaj7, and the I chord is Cmaj7.

The original rhythm of the melody has essentially been preserved, and in that sense, it is still quite simple. Perform the arrangement slowly, with a gentle touch, to maximize the pretty sounds of the expanded jazz harmony. The arrangement could also be played *rubato*, i.e., in free time.

As Summer Leaves

As Summer Leaves is based on the chord progression from a Jazz Standard, *Autumn Leaves* written by Joseph Kosma in 1945, lyrics by Johnny Mercer.

The harmony provides a "must know" chord progression for jazz musicians. This progression is referred to as the: "ii-V-I." Two examples of the ii-V-I progression in this song are: Am-D7-Gmaj7; and F♯m7(♭5)-B7-Em.

Be sure to bring out the melody by keeping the chords in the background. One example is in bars 5 and 13. Here, you'll need to use your first finger to barre the F♯m7(♭5) chord across all four strings, which will allow the A melody note ring over the chords. Also be aware in bars 8, 16, and 33 that the E bass note on the sixth string and the E melody note on the fourth string will need to be "hybrid picked." That is, use your pick to play the low E, and use a finger (2nd or 3rd tend to work well) on your pick hand to play the high E.

In bars 26-27, even though the chord moves up the neck and the name changes from E♭dim7 to F♯dim7 to Adim7, notice that it's the same "shape." Planing diminished 7 or dominant 7♭9 chords is a common "trick" jazz guitarists use.

In the Bridge section, carefully observe the rests so there is an obvious contrast between the chords being played forte, and the rests as a period of silence.

C&R Blues

C&R stands for "Call & Response," and the main theme of the piece is a call and response between the melody and harmony. The form is a 12-bar blues, an ideal form for call and response.

Most of the melody is a two-bar "riff," a short musical phrase. The primary pattern is that the riff is played in the first two bars of every 4-bar phrase, and then the response is played in the last two bars of every 4-bar phrase. To break it down, the main riff happens in bars 1-2— the call. Then in bars 3-4, the harmony answers the riff— the response. The riff from bars 1-2 is then transposed up a perfect 4th and repeated in bar 5-6. Bars 9 introduces a new riff, and bar 10 repeats it down a whole step. Bar 11 then uses a variation of the main riff from bar 1, and bar 12 issues the response. To better convey the call and response, play the calls louder and the responses softer. Think of yourself as a piano player— the calls are with your right hand, and the responses are with your left hand.

A technique used here is playing the melody in octaves, as in bars 2 and 6. This thickens out what would otherwise be a single-note melody. It's a handy technique to break up the overall texture of single notes and chords.

Bars 13-24— the second chorus— repeat the entire melody from bars 1-12 but include some rhythmic variation. For instance, an extra eighth note is added to bars 13-14 and 16. Also, an extra chord, Gm9, is added to bar 16 to "tonicize" (make a chord a temporary tonic or I chord) the F9 in bar 17— Gm9-C13-F9. Bars 25-32, the ending, tag the melody in bars 21-24. To create interest in these bars, experiment with different volumes. For example, you could play bars 25-28 soft, get loud in bars 29-31, and play the final bar, 32, soft.

Greensleeves

Greensleeves has been adopted into the Christian music tradition and is sometimes known as *What Child Is This?* But it's really an old English folk song with a pretty melody and simple harmony, which has been expanded for this arrangement. The feel here is a jazz waltz (3/4 time) with swing eighth notes. The arrangement opens with an 8-bar introduction that emphasizes the A to F♯ relationship, creating a "modal" feeling, as in bars 2, 4, 6, and 8. The mode here is A Dorian, which is a G major scale starting and ending on A— ABCDEF♯GA. But starting on A creates a new mood or "mode," which helps give *Greensleeves* its haunting character. The open G string against the fretted F♯ in bars 2 and 6 creates a "rub" and accentuates the haunting quality of the piece. Overall, the arrangement plays on the use of open strings against fretted chords.

The key is allowing as many chords to ring as possible. Not every last possible hold is notated, so you are encouraged to experiment and hold chords for longer than written.

One interesting feature is in bars 25-28 and 33-36, which have the same melody and harmony but use "variation." Bar 33 uses a straight C triad instead of the C(add9) in bar 25, and bar 34 uses a C♯dim7 instead of the C(add9) in bar 26. Variation, even slight, is a handy technique to create interest when an element— melody, harmony, rhythm— is repeated.

Nine Miles From Home

This ballad has a simple, folk-like melody, mostly in half notes and quarter notes. It moves along gently but assuredly. There are multiple chords that "skip a string" in the voicing, for example the F/A in bar 1, the Dm7 in bar 6, and the F♯7(♯11) in bar 8. Pick "through" the skipped string as if it weren't there. The resulting effect will sound slightly percussive, because you're picking a string that has no pitch. Having a skipped string in voicings is quite common in jazz, so it's valuable to learn this technique. Another method to playing chords with skipped strings is to fingerpick them. You might try this for part or all of the piece.

The key to achieving a lush sound here is to let the chords ring for their full value. Smoothly connect one chord to the next, lifting your fingers only at the last possible fraction of a second before switching to the next chord. There are a lot of bass notes and voicings on the lower strings, so your left hand might get fatigued. Take your time, and rest when you need to. Shake out your left hand. Keep working steadily through the piece over time. It's good for building left-hand endurance.

Shenandoah

Shenandoah comes from the American folk song tradition. It has a beautifully pure melody, and its original harmony is in simple triads. This chord melody adds some passing chords as well as extensions and altered notes that give it a jazz flavor. The arrangement begins with an 8-bar introduction to set the tone. The melody begins at measure 9.

Most of the melody is in long, simple rhythms. Things move a little faster rhythmically and harmonically from bar 22-26. Watch the voicings here and work through them slowly. In particular, the chords in bars 25-26 use smooth voice leading and will make sense as you learn them. The arrangement slows down at bar 27 to recap the introduction as an ending.

Silent Night

The music to this Christmas Classic was composed on the guitar by Franz Gruber in 1818. Joseph Mohr, a church organist, had already written the lyrics. The story goes that just before Christmas, Mohr gave the lyrics to Gruber and asked him if he could write a melody for his lyrics to be performed on Christmas Eve. So a few days later Silent Night was first performed on a snowy Christmas Eve featuring a vocalist accompanied by a guitar.

This arrangement is simplistic in its approach by adding new voicings to the harmony. For example, major chords are transformed into maj7's or (add)9's, which provide a more elegant sound to the basic harmony. The addition of color tones (9ths and 13ths) entice the listeners ears to the new harmony. Notice the chord substitutions used in bars 10 and 14, along with a descending bass line leading to the I chord A.

Overall, you will need to fingerpick this piece because most of the chords have "string skips" in them. For example, all four-string chords, like the A(add9) in bar 1, would be played with your thumb on the lowest note and your index, middle, and ring fingers on the highest three notes. In bar 7, the A6 on beat 1 could be played with the thumb and index and middle, or you could strum this chord with your thumb, since the notes are all on adjacent strings. There are also other chords in this arrangement that could be strummed. Experiment with different fingerpicking combinations to find ones that make the most sense for individual chords.

There are a couple of tricky spots to watch out for. One is in bar 14, from C#m7 to Bm7/E. The fingering will take some time to master. Another spot is in bar 23. Watch your fingerpicking on this A arpeggio— the F# is on a lower string than the E's, forming something of an "aural illusion."

As in other places in this book, the diminished 7 or dominant 7♭9 chords are "planed," that is, they use the same shape moving up or down the neck. You'll see this in bar 18.

The use of pedal point in the first and second endings gives a contrast to the general serene sounds that precede, leading into a gentle ending. Keeping with the Christmas spirit, musicians often end a holiday tune with a hint of *Jingle Bells*, which usually brings a smile to the listener's faces.

Swanee River

Stephen Foster wrote this famous melody about a river in Florida, even though he never visited "The Sunshine State." *Swanee River* is arranged as a ballad. The term "with expression" in the tempo indicates that the performer can slightly vary the tempo for dramatic or expressive purposes. Be sure to use the fermatas to add even more expression. The harmonic structure of this arrangement is much different than the original, so be sure that each note of the chords is clear and concise.

There are a couple of jumps to watch out for. In bar 3, F#m7 to C#m7 leaps up the guitar by three frets and three strings. Take your time and work on this slowly, noticing how your fingers move from one shape to the next. It will come with practice. In bar 11, the E7 chord on the 12th fret to the C note on the 8th fret of the first string may seem odd to finger with your 4th finger. But using your 4th finger will help you transition into the A#dim7 in bar 12 more easily, since the 4th finger is used on the first string in this chord.

In bar 18, you'll notice the B9 chord is quite high on the neck. Don't freak out! This is a shape you've already played in bar 6, F#9. Also notice that the same shape is used for all the m7 chords in bars 21-24. In addition, in bar 30, barre your first finger across all four strings, a prep which will make it easier to "catch" the E note on beat 2.

To a Wild Rose

This famous song was written for piano by Edward MacDowell in 1896. It is one of the first Americana songs, containing melodies from Native American themes. *To a Wild Rose* is very expressive song, similar in style to *Swanee River* on page 16. Your tempo can "bend" as you weave your way through the harmonies. Don't be in a hurry.

You can see that there are not many notes in this song, the chords voicing are rather sparse, many times there only three or four notes. Melodies like this should alert you that every note counts, so be sure that you can hear every note. The tempo is slow enough so you do not have to rush the tempo at any time.

In bar 12 on the B13 chord, use your 3rd finger to barre the A and C# notes on the second and third strings. It will make this chord much easier to play than using all four fingers. In bars 25-28, the various E7 and E9 chords use some classic jazz guitar voicings that come up frequently. Work through them slowly until you can play each shape and transition from one to the next seamlessly.

G1056